Other Books by Nicklaus Suino

The Drinking Game

Budo Mind and Body: Training Secrets of the Japanese Martial Arts (comprehensive revision of *Arts of Strength, Arts of Serenity*)

Arts of Strength, Arts of Serenity

Strategy in Japanese Swordsmanship

Practice Drills for Japanese Swordsmanship

The Art of Japanese Swordsmanship

101 Ideas to Kick Your Ass into Gear (with Ian Gray)

Success Sandbox (with Ian Gray)

SEO and Beyond: How to Rocket Your Website to Page One of Google! (with Don E. Prior III)

LOOK UP!

LOOK UP!

**Inspiration and Action for
Challenging Times**

by Nicklaus Suino

**MASTER
&FOOL**

Ann Arbor, Michigan

Master and Fool, LLC
2875 Boardwalk, Suite H
Ann Arbor, Michigan 48108

10 9 8 7 6 5 4 3 2 1

FIRST EDITION

Written, Edited, and Printed in the
United States of America

ISBN-10: 0692810595
ISBN-13: 978-0692810590

Every day, I step into a world of unlimited possibility. I get to choose how much of that possibility is manifested in my life, and the lives of those around me.

Cover photo by Paul Fisher.

To Charly "Sir Charles" Caldwell,
for helping so many people to look up.

Keep your eyes on the stars and your feet on the ground.

- Theodore Roosevelt

One - How's Your Life?

Is your life everything you want it to be?

Is there a disconnect between where you are right now and where you wish you could be if just a few more things went right?

Do you keep feeling that things really, truly could be better?

If you're like most people, there are probably a few things about your life that you'd like to change. Maybe there are a *lot* of things you'd change! It can be challenging and exhausting to get up, day after day, and keep facing the same kinds of problems over and over.

Wouldn't it be refreshing to find a path to solving at least some of the things that keep you from living the life you want, finding the love you want, or leaving your mark on the world the way you believe you're here on earth to do?

Even the most successful people would probably change at least a few things about the way they live. Maybe they'd like to help more people. Maybe they're frustrated by the time they have to spend doing trivial tasks. Maybe they'd like their personal interactions to be deeper. Maybe they'd like to spend more time in nature with nothing on their "to-do" list.

The key for high performing people is that they *do* find ways to change. If they want small improvements, they make adjustments to what they look for, what they do, and how they interact with others to get closer to their ideal way of living. If they want major change, they often seek out powerful role models; people who are already very good at the things they want to be good at or who can help them improve.

Sometimes, if they simply want to do a better job of living up to their own ideals, they "look up" to their own most positive thoughts, words or actions and put more focus on living in accord with them. You can make an incredible difference in your own life by seeking out role models, finding inspiration, and focusing on the better angels of your nature.

When you want to live a richer, more energetic, more fulfilled life ... look up!

Opportunities are Everywhere

It's been said that opportunities are everywhere; that we just have to learn how to see them. Examples and guidance for how to live a richer, more exciting, more passionate and more fulfilling life are indeed all around us. Sometimes they're "above" us in some way – people who are happier than we are, people who are more effective, men with more money, women with more influence, or spiritual leaders who contribute in profound ways to the improvement of humankind.

Sometimes what we need is to focus on our own thoughts "up" where we keep our most productive, positive ideas about ourselves, about others, about humanity, or about the planet.

Sometimes opportunity is "up" spiritually. If you're religious or spiritual, you can look up to your clergy, to inspirational stories from your religious texts, or to your private conversations with the almighty.

Look for these opportunities and you'll begin to find them. When you find them, there lies the start of your own journey!

Imagine Your Life ...

Imagine what your life would be like if you had the habit of reflexively turning toward success in all things, both small and large. What if that habit was so deeply ingrained that, whenever you had a decision to make, your choice was positive, productive, and effective? Whether small or large, if your decisions reflected the wisdom of the ages (or at least the wisdom of somebody who has already gotten where you want to go), by multiplying effort on top of effort, you could get yourself on a parabolic path toward the life you wish for, the life of your dreams, full of passion, energy, and purpose!

Imagine, too, the effect that approach to life would have not just on how *you* live, but on the lives of those around you. If your family was swept up in your upward spiral and they, too, lived with more effectiveness and joy, would that change their experience of the world? If the people you work with saw positive change happening to you and began to make similar changes to their own approach, living with more joy, improving their circumstances, and influencing their family and friends for the better, would that change your workplace?

How amazing could your world become?

Do you realize that by taking a few simple steps and building a few simple habits you could not only begin moving toward the life of your dreams, you could create incredible positive change not just for those around you, but those around *them* too, and maybe start to change the world?

Awesome vision, right?

How does it all start? By looking up!

LOOK UP!

Notes

Notes

LOOK UP!

If you can dream it, you can do it.

- Walt Disney

Two - How's Your Job?

Do you dread going to work?

Are you stuck in a job that's below your potential, with no obvious way to move up, move over, or move out?

Is your work just "okay," something you drag yourself to for the money, but for which you have no passion?

Do you want to get ahead at work? To start getting the attention you deserve? To earn a good living, to make a difference in your company or your community, and to step into a title that others will view with respect?

You can start by looking up!

When You Look Up

When you look up and see who in your company has managed to rise above the futility of the same position, the same work, the same problems day after day, you can start to explore why they are different, how they were able to ascend, and what they did that separates them from those who aren't able to change.

Look up to the people in your company who've made it to positions that you'd like to have. Look up to the most effective people, be they engineers, secretaries, administrators or managers. Look up to the people in the "C" suite. Look to the founders of the company. Look up to a boss who's interested in grooming new talent, look up to business coaches, look up to mentors or a mentorship group.

Look up and see who's moved up by leaving the company altogether, and you may learn what you need to do to take the next step in your own career, even if that means that you, too, have to leave. If you're contemplating getting out of the rat race and actually getting into business for yourself, look up to successful entrepreneurs who have started businesses like the one you aspire to start. Look up to networking opportunities, business relationships and startup incubators.

Look In

One of the key things to pay attention to in your role models is their "why?" Figure out their intrinsic reasons for wanting to excel. Despite all the advantages of money, status, and influence, the "why?" is usually a much more powerful motivator for people in the long run.

When people rise for extrinsic reasons, their lives are often devoid of any sense of meaning and connectedness. Some will sabotage themselves after reaching a high level because there's no deeper reason to for them to be there.

On the other hand, people with a powerful "why" are often able to maintain their drive day after day, month after month, year after year, even when the going is very tough, when there are few extrinsic rewards, and when what they want to achieve seems incredibly distant. A powerful internal drive informs many of their decisions, both big and small, and can lead them to make better choices even when they don't fully understand the problems they may face.

Your own "why?" can be both a compass and an engine. Time you spend getting to the deepest motivations of your role models or yourself will not be wasted.

A word of warning, however: getting to people's deepest motivations is not always easy. Those motivations are often tied to formative experiences that were traumatic or otherwise deeply emotional. Your role models may not want to share such personal information in a business environment, especially if they don't know you well.

A big part of looking up is building trust. To understand your boss, the founder, or your business mentor, you'll have to listen, to ask gentle, open-ended questions, and to be truly sincere in your interest in them and their path to success. And you'll have to treat the information you get as sacrosanct. The usual workplace gossiping and vying for position do not apply to these relationships – you have to maintain strict respect and confidence if you want to build deep relationships.

As you get to know more people in positions that you may want to occupy one day, be prepared to find out that their "why?" may not be the same as yours. That's okay. What's important is that you understand how theirs motivates them and informs their decision making; how it provides the energy for how they achieve and what they do, or have done.

Look Back

As you engage in this process you may have to do some "looking back" of your own to figure out where your motivations come from. Knowing what drives you – truly knowing rather than just accepting expectations: society's, your friends', your parents' – is very powerful. When you understand it, you will be able to use it not only as a source of energy, but also as a navigation tool.

Knowing who you are provides you with a spiritual compass. It helps you navigate through the complex world of business toward the position you believe you should rightfully occupy. When you stray from what truly matters to you, you'll likely find that you're less happy, that it takes a lot more effort to achieve, and that you experience a lot more stress. When you act in accord with your true motivations, you'll find that you're happier, more effective, and more relaxed.

Imagine finding a great mentor within your company, somebody who has achieved greatly, who is generous in spirit, and who is willing to share a little time with you every week or two. You look up to them as a role model. You "look in" to learn why they act as they do and how to apply some of their thinking to your own decisions and actions.

You "look back" to learn what truly works to motivate you to do your best. Little by little, you start to make better choices at work, develop better relationships, get noticed more often by the right people for the right reasons. Can you feel how much difference this could make for your career if you apply it consistently, week after week, month after month, year after year?

Look to the Work

People seem to overestimate how much difference they can make in a few months. There are lots of moving parts. Some people will work against you, including the skeptics and those whose agendas are different from yours. It also simply takes time to navigate around obstacles and shift the world to serve your higher aims. Hang in there until you begin to see the change you want!

People also seem to vastly underestimate how much difference they can make in a few years. The "look up" concept of getting both the small things and large things right and doing so consistently over a long period of time is very powerful. When your confidence drops, look up to your vision of how your career will look when you *do* achieve your goals, regardless of how long it takes or how much work is involved. It's going to be okay. Things worth doing are worth working for!

Look up to your friends in higher places to see that, though there are challenges at every level, change need not be feared. Listen ... you'll have to work at work no matter which floor your office is on, so you may as well enjoy the perks of being closer to the top, and you'll have a better chance of helping more people from a higher vantage point. Look up to the people who help you keep faith in your ability to thrive, who help you paint a vivid picture of your success. Hard work is a lot easier if you're clear about what you want it to bring you.

When you develop the habit of looking up, of making positive and productive choices more and more often, change will come to you. Living to your higher self at work will become a habit, and you'll transform yourself into someone who gets things done, a problem solver, a resource for others, and perhaps even a mentor to those who haven't yet achieved your level.

No matter what you do for a living, no matter the title on your door, no matter the size of your paycheck, that's a nice place to be.

It all starts by looking up!

Notes

LOOK UP!

Notes

You are not here merely to make a living. You are here in order to enable the world to live more amply, with greater vision, with a finer spirit of hope and achievement. You are here to enrich the world, and you impoverish yourself if you forget the errand.

- Woodrow Wilson

LOOK UP!

Three - How Well Do You Treat People?

Do you value other people as much as you should?

Do you ever have those moments where you think, "I should really start being nicer to people"?

Have you ever mistreated somebody close to you, then regretted it later? Most of us have!

Can you imagine a world in which you're conscious of the value and connectedness of each and every person you meet? In which you interact with them in a way that truly validates their existence?

If you're having trouble living up to your own ideals of how to interact with people, look up!

Looking in the Wrong Direction?

Look up to the friends in your life who are especially kind to you. Look up to teachers you've had who, with a gentle word or gesture, have given you a sense of worth or self-assurance. Look up to business people who, having created empires, have also found ways to give back or empower not just a few, but many, many people. Look up to spiritual leaders who have sacrificed themselves to help communities, nations or the world accede to new levels of awareness and humanity. Examples are everywhere if you look in the right direction!

It's true, there are places you could look that would not inspire you. If you look to friends who are cynical or judgmental, you won't find yourself inspired to treat them with the utmost respect or kindness. If you focus on that one teacher you had who was harsh or negative, you'll likely recall your feelings of humiliation or inadequacy instead of his or her skill at educating students. If you think only of greedy or exploitive business people, you may end up believing that financial success only happens on the backs of the less fortunate. If you pay attention to the politicians or cause-baiters who show up only when there's a chance to flog their message and drive a wedge between people, you may think humanity is lost.

But beware, when you're looking in the direction of people like that, you're looking down. It's an easy trap to fall into because the bad examples tend to get more press. Looking down is useful to remind you what behavior to avoid, but when you want to level up, look up!

It can be Simple

It sounds simple because it is. Perhaps not *easy*, but simple. Most of us are social creatures, and we respond to the people around us. If you're struggling to treat people well, it can get a lot easier if you hang around with others who treat you well. You pay attention to their actions and return the favor with a kind word or deed. Repeated actions become habits, and you may soon be a lot closer to the kind of person you yourself would like to hang around with!

Sure, you'll backslide. If you're prone to crankiness, you're going to have occasional bad moments. If your jokes sometimes veer into insults or spiteful comments, it may take a while to retrain your brain to stick with supportive words. Sometimes you'll be tired or frustrated and it will be all you can do to keep your eyes open and put one foot in front of the other, much less focus on examples of positive, supportive behavior. But you can start by asking yourself, "am I looking up?"

Where the Magic Happens

Here's the crazy "magic" about this way of thinking: looking down or looking up is really just a mindset. Seek and ye shall find. If you're looking for the negative, you'll probably find it even in the nicest people. "Hey, I don't like the way that person does her hair!" But is that really the kind of person *you* want to be, the kind who focuses on the faults of others? It shall not profit a man to find a thousand faults in others, but a single blessing may point the way to his kingdom!

If you're looking up instead, you may find that you can be inspired by the very same person in whom you found a negative character trait. After all, like the rest of us, he or she is made up of both gifts and challenges. "Wow, she is an amazing event organizer. Look at the passion she pours into her work. She makes her love for humanity manifest by creating great events."

Now that's the kind of thing you'd like to notice about somebody! And if you see it, why not say it? "I just love the passion you pour into your work. It inspires me!" Telling your friend something so positive may give her a jolt of connectedness and energy that changes her day for the better, not to mention how great it could make you feel.

It's inspiring even to write these words, to know that sharing the simplest of ideas with just a few people might help you find a way to treat the people around you just a little better, with the hope that you experience more joy and that your friends and family do, too!

Stay Humble and Kind

A key quality that helps with treating people well is humility. We all have reason to be humble. After all, there are over seven billion people in the world, and each of us is just one among many. We all have something to offer, but we also have much to improve upon. Even if you're a well actualized human being, comfortable in your own skin and relatively successful, that doesn't mean your work is done. There are countless areas to work on. Understanding your own need for self-improvement can help with humility.

Empty your cup. Proceed with an open heart and a willing mind, and not only will you find that it's easier to treat others well, but you may find that you see more opportunities to succeed than you would if you believe you already have everything figured out.

How does it all start? By looking up!

Notes

Notes

LOOK UP!

Do the difficult things while they are easy and do the great things while they are small. A journey of a thousand miles must begin with a single step.

- Lao Tzu

Four - How's Your Diet?

Do you have a few extra pounds you'd really like to shed?

Do you struggle to make healthy choices at the table?

Does your diet keep you from feeling that you're reaching your potential?

If you want to finally start eating better, to finally feel good each and every day, to be charged with energy and have the focus you need to stay productive at work, engaged with your family, and focused on your personal mission, start by looking up!

Did You Save Room for Dessert?

We're bombarded with thousands of ways to fail at eating. Unless you totally retreat from society, you're probably exposed to ads for unhealthy foods countless times each day. They come at you on TV, on websites, on billboards, in magazines, in snack aisles, and in that frequently-asked-question just when you've once again overeaten at the dinner table:

"Did you save room for dessert?"

Let's face it, almost nobody "saves" room for dessert. Instead, we cram every tasty morsel into our mouths until our pants are ready to burst. That should more than satisfy us, but we find a way to pile even more sweet, high calorie junk on top of what is already way too much for a normal human, then we wash it all down with a coma-inducing beverage or two.

Where were we looking? *Down* at the menu, right?

If you want to start taking control of what your hands put in your mouth, it may be time to start using your brain to point your eyes in a different direction.

Look up to your healthiest friends and ask them how they manage energy-positive eating. Look up to the athletes you admire – almost everybody in sports these days does an interview about how they eat to excel.

Look up to the positive role models who offer dietary programs for sale. Sure, they're trying to make money, but most programs are at least partly based on good fundamentals, so keep the good and ignore the rest.

Look up sound dietary science by reading a few actual books on the subject. Look up to the people who are living for a purpose greater than themselves, those who are working to help humanity. How do they fuel themselves for such important missions?

How are They Doing it?

Have you taken the time to imagine how a life of looking up would be? Have you really set everything aside, taken a few deep breaths, closed your eyes, and imagined what things will be like when you've made a habit of looking up, of making productive choices, of focusing on the positive?

Exciting, isn't it? A little dreaming is a great way to get started on monumental personal change!

But what if you find out that your "fit" friend is really not that healthy, and is engaging in some unhealthy practice like taking stimulants or binging and purging?

What if you find out that super fit athlete whose stats you follow like they were the Colonel's secret recipe is taking steroids? What if your celebrity health guru is dispensing garbage advice? (Some do.) What if scientists discover that the "healthy eating" dogma of the past four decades was flawed? What if the reason the guru or savior seems so healthy has nothing at all to do with dietary choices, but comes from his or her inner passion and devotion to the cause?

Challenging questions. Now we're getting somewhere! Are you ready to take the next step in your personal evolution? Should you just give up and do what other people do, even when it's deeply flawed? Of course not. You're better than that. Once you've seen the truth, you know that looking to a person who's not actually doing what you want to do for inspiration or advice would not be looking up. He is not a successful role model; it would be looking down. So look elsewhere.

Inspiration is all around you if you train your eyes to see it.

Build a Routine

Resolve to look up, commit to it, and make it a habit so your choices are better all day, every day. That lets you start creating enormous change for yourself, your family and your community. Your changes will probably be incremental, and they'll take time to add up, but they will happen and it's a lot of fun when they do.

Remember, the key to meaningful change is looking up. If your athlete hero is taking steroids, does looking to her constitute "looking up"? If that famous internet diet celebrity is spouting nonsense that's unsupported by science, is following her "looking up"? If the best science discovers that a low fat, carbohydrate-based diet is not good for you as they've been saying for forty years, but that instead a high fat, high fiber regimen is much more likely to help you lose weight and avoid disease, would it make sense to keep stuffing fat free muffins in your face for breakfast?

You can't just check out and take a robotic approach to becoming a happier, healthier, more amazing person. Just because you showered today doesn't mean you don't have to shower tomorrow. Just because you slept last night doesn't mean you won't have to sleep tonight.

It's the same with looking up. Just because you looked up yesterday doesn't mean you don't have to look up today. You start by looking for good role models, but you need to confirm the quality of your choices from time to time. Check in on who and what you're looking up to. If you get information that shows you the direction you're looking is not productive, then it's time to reset, find better examples or role models, and once again start looking up!

Do Even More

In fact, you can and should do even more.

Once you get in the habit of looking up – of finding great role models, studying what they do, how they do it, and how they think about what they do – you'll get into a positive spiral of personal improvement. You'll check in from time to time to make sure your role models are still worth following. You'll think carefully about your choices and make sure you're truly using what you've learned to move in the direction of your dreams.

It's a powerful way to keep yourself on a positive, productive path. But guess what? When all this works out, you'll find that the more you look up, the higher you may have to look.

You need new role models as you become more and more successful. What got you here may not get you there. That's okay, but it does mean you have to add a step to your framework of personal improvement habits. That step is making sure you're looking up to the right examples for where you are *right now*.

In the beginning, if you started out struggling just to wean yourself off fast food, your role models were probably those who could help you learn to make just a few more healthy choices each day. But if you stay on the path to healthy, vibrant living long enough, you might find yourself eating for performance – maybe you start running marathons, doing Olympic lifting or leading aerobic dance classes – and you need specific guidance on how to reach new levels of strength, energy or recovery. That requires a different kind of inspiration.

If you're now striving to achieve at a much higher level, you may need to be much more disciplined to feed your body and mind for recovery and focus. And your palate might accept food choices that would have seemed horrible when you started.

A Habit of Constant Improvement

The power of embracing what you need to go from where you are now to where you want to be tomorrow is enormous. The highest performers have figured out how to operate this way – to not only follow their immediate role models, but to always be on the lookout for better inspiration and more effective guidance. It keeps them in a state of constant improvement. Over time, it gives them the leverage to live in ways that are difficult for the rest of us to imagine. It's challenging to live that way at first, but it's vibrant and full of rewards, both extrinsic and intrinsic.

So many people just "wish" they could change, and end up in a long, slow spiral of losing mobility and gaining weight. It blocks them from the extraordinary life they could be living. They wish for change but don't commit to it ... or simply don't know how to start. You don't have to be like that. Each passing decade can be a disappointment or a delight; which one is up to you. Take control of what you put into your mouth, and you'll be amazed at what you can get out of your body and your mind.

LOOK UP!

If you're struggling to make healthy food choices, don't just wish for change. Find role models, coaches, programs, or friends who can help you develop more energy-positive thoughts and behaviors. You can accomplish amazing things with the right influences around you.

Start by looking up!

Notes

LOOK UP!

Notes

What you get by achieving your goals is not as important as what you become by achieving your goals.

- Zig Ziglar

Five - How's Your Charity?

Are you frustrated with all the poverty in the world?

Does reading about people who can't get good food or a good education stab at your heart?

Does it drive you crazy to see other people suffering day after day, year after year, without having the time or the tools to help them change their circumstances?

Can you imagine yourself in a role that allows you to provide much needed help for the disadvantaged?

Are you waiting for that "one thing" that, if only you had it, you could truly start to change the fortunes of people less well off than you?

As much good as there is in the world, there are still a lot of people suffering needlessly. Sensitive human beings understand that there are things they can do to help, and there are a lot of people like you who are deeply frustrated that more isn't being done.

At the same time, many of us who could make a real difference for needy people don't do it because we think it's too difficult, or because we don't know how to get started. It's quite possible that, to be a little more charitable, all you need is some inspiration and guidance.

You could start by looking up!

A Deep Sense of Satisfaction

Look up to a friend or relative who always seems to be doing something to help others. Look up to the charity organizer at work who's constantly arranging fund raisers or food drives. Look up to the leader of a local helping organization. Look up to celebrities who are known for giving to good causes. Look up to businesses that have a charitable purpose built into their charters. Look up to people who make it their mission to live a charitable life, who have made helping those in need the very purpose of their existence.

If you're one of those people who gets a deep sense of satisfaction from giving, imagine the warmth and connectedness you'll feel when you've developed a habit of seeking out opportunities to help others. Imagine the good you can do when you get identified as the "go-to" person at work for charitable events.

Imagine how you can scale up your helping impulses by aligning with a local charitable organization to reach the needy in your city or town. Imagine how much more good you can do by joining your efforts with those of someone who's known for helping disadvantaged people all over the world.

Let yourself dream a little about starting or running a business that not only makes money, but also donates a share of every dollar as an integral part of what it does. Imagine the power of giving your life to helping, to making it your purpose to uplift others by teaching them how to get out of poverty.

Now that would be a life worth living!

Easing the suffering of others is rewarding for its own sake, but it can also be an amazing tool for focusing the energy of groups of people. When you strike the right chord, letting people know that they're capable of making a difference, they will work extremely hard to help. You can organize people, get things done, have fun, make a difference, and actually create real change – within a family, in a church, in a school, in a business, or in a community.

When your effort and ideas catch fire, you could help change a huge part of the world.

Start by looking up.

You Are a Force for Good

In this, as in all things, you'll have false starts and failures. Those should not deter you … changing the flow of human events can take time! To get past the obstacles, be sure you're starting with the right role models. Find the person who inspires you, figure out what they're doing and why they're doing it. Decide how you can do something similar with your means and circumstances. Then do it.

Now you're on your way!

Keep your eyes open, of course. When you make a habit of giving to others, you'll encounter people and groups that take a lot and give little. When you see that happening, dig deeper. If it turns out that one of your role models or mentors is not truly giving, then you'll know that looking to them is looking down. That's the wrong direction. Time to find another source of inspiration!

This habit, like focusing on your life's mission or becoming truly vibrant, is scalable. The better you get at it, the higher you can reach. The higher you reach, the more opportunities you'll find to help even more people. You've read the stories and seen the news about powerful people who truly change the world with their giving. They often start out just like any ordinary person.

That person can be you.

But nobody has ever taken the second step without taking the first step first, and as long as you haven't taken the first step, you're stuck in place. Stuck is not the place you want to be. You want to be in the game. You want your eyes open for opportunity. You want to be the agent of powerful change. You, yes you, have the potential to be a force for good, to become a giving machine, to help the people around you and maybe people all over the world.

It's going to be amazing.

And it starts by looking up!

LOOK UP!

Notes

Notes

LOOK UP!

Either you run the day or the day runs you.

- Jim Rohn

Six - How's Your Fitness?

Could you be in better shape?

Are you frustrated with your cycle of training for a few days, a few weeks, or a month, then falling off the treadmill, so to speak, and failing to get to the gym for months?

Can you see your potential for improved fitness, better energy, and a more positive attitude if only you could stick to a workout regimen?

When you want to get in shape, when you want to finally, finally, finally get fit and get off the cycle of excuses and missing your goals, look up! Look up to friends who seem to get out running every day or get to the gym consistently. Look up to the fitness gurus who offer training routines on DVDs or on YouTube. Look up to people around you who attend organized events like triathalons, Tough Mudders, grappling tournaments or CrossFit Games to help them stay motivated and keep them training. Look up to leaders of gyms or dojos who provide a place to train, a framework for you to work in and the motivation for you to stay fit. Look up to famous athletes or fitness figures who provide inspiration with their accomplishments.

It starts by looking up.

You find a role model or inspirational figure, study them to figure out what they do and how they do it, and start doing it yourself. That can get you back in the gym, back on the running trail, back in the dojo, or back into the "box."

But the best benefits of training, whether you do weight lifting, running, martial arts, Crossfit, or jazz dance, come when you stick with it over the long term. It may take more than simply looking up to a role model to find a routine you like. You may have to find a source of continuous inspiration, which is where a trainer, coach, or *Sensei* is often useful. If there's someone in your life you can look up to for fitness guidance, techniques, inspiration, and even companionship, that could be the next level for you.

Stick with It

Starting a training routine can be the most difficult time. You're not good at the motions. The training space is unfamiliar. Your muscles aren't used to the particular exertion required. You don't know exactly what to focus on or what mindsets are most helpful.

After the excitement of the first few days wears off, there's often a period of a few weeks or months when you're not fully into the routine. That's when people tend to quit, which is too bad, because if they stayed with it just a little longer, they'd likely learn the routine and build good habits that would stay with them for the long term.

It's after you've mastered the basics that you can get into the flow, really enjoy the training, benefit from it, and focus on the things that will help change your life!

If you're already involved in some form of fitness activity at a high level, you understand. You go through an established warm up routine with the right expectations, and even if you're a little tired or lacking in motivation, by the time you get through your warm up and basics, you're ready for the heart of your training.

Get Totally Engaged

Maybe you're striving for a personal best on bench press. You've gradually increased your 2-3 rep max and today you're trying to add just one more pound. There's anticipation and excitement as you get fired up to push that much weight. If you get under the bar and you're in the right frame of mind, you've gotten enough sleep, you're hydrated and you've got the proper carb load, you're going to drive through what seems like an impossible barrier and move that mountain of iron, and it's going to feel amazing. And if you properly feed yourself and recover, virtually every muscle in your body will grow for a week!

Maybe you're trying to add distance to your run to prepare for a race. You've got a course mapped out that's two miles longer than your average, you're up early, you're feeling loose, you've stretched well, and as you take ten deep breaths to get your heart rate up, you can feel the trail pulling you forward. You know there's a half marathon or a Tough Mudder next month and this will be your first run at the distance you need. You jog past rabbits and deer in the fields and you hear birds chirping as you glide by. At your best moments, in the smooth activity of the moment and the anticipation of the challenge ahead, running is like soaring through the air. It's completely rewarding for its own sake.

Maybe you're preparing for a judo tournament.
You've achieved brown belt after three years of train-
ing, you've won matches at a few tournaments, and now
you're committed to being fully prepared for the next
big one. Your body's in shape, your nutrition is good,
you have a team of support in your dojo, and you've
developed two throws that work together as an effective
combination. You show up for the *randori* (sparring)
session, make your bows of respect, run through your
warm up, and begin with a few sets of practice setups.

You play a couple of light rounds with one or two
training partners, then turn to that one guy or gal who
gives you so much trouble, your nemesis, the training
partner who's close to you in size and talent, but who
for some reason is the one person you just get the most
satisfaction out of competing against. You bow, step for-
ward, get your grip, and all at once you're totally in the
game, fully immersed in the moment, deeply engaged
in the physical and mental chess match that is the best
sort of judo! Maybe you throw first, maybe your training
partner throws you first, but whatever happens, you're
living within the intense, energetic world of judo and
thinking about absolutely nothing else!

These are examples of the kind of joy you can get from being in a state of flow in your fitness activity ... when you're being challenged enough so that you're totally consumed with your training and when you've been in the game long enough that your body and mind are capable of playing at that level for sustained periods.

You start by looking up. To stay in it long enough to play at a high level with joy, you may need to look up to someone who is not only good at what you want to be good at, but who is also good at leading and motivating you. That's the next level of looking up. Imagine having someone in your corner who's walked the road you're walking, who cares about your success, who can guide and motivate you, and who can keep you from making big mistakes as you raise your fitness level.

As we said, that can be the role of the coach, Sensei, or mentor. Sometimes it's just the person in the gym who's been training longer than you. They can give you a word of encouragement or a pat on the back. When you start looking, you'll find that people who can inspire or guide you are everywhere.

LOOK UP!

If you're trying to improve – or just trying to get started – don't wait to start looking. The human body is wired for improvement ... and life is better when you recognize that and get started on your own mission. Find what you were meant to do and you may end up being your own best source of guidance and inspiration.

Start by looking up!

Notes

LOOK UP!

Notes

Whatever you want in life, other people are going to want it too. Believe in yourself enough to accept the idea that you have an equal right to it.

- Diane Sawyer

Seven - How Are Your Finances?

Are you tired of constantly having to say "someday" when it comes to your dreams?

Do you wish your income, for once, was a little bigger than your bills? Maybe a lot bigger?

Do you dream of finding a way to increase your savings and still have a significant vacation once a year?

The majority of people in the US are living paycheck to paycheck. One financial emergency could drive most families into bankruptcy. So many of us struggle to put a little money into savings, not to mention trying to feel comfortable enough to take a long vacation or do something special for our families. It would probably help you feel a lot lighter if you were able to get ahead of your bills, wouldn't it? If you had money set aside for emergencies, a little in an investment account, and perhaps a small (or not so small) vacation fund, would that help change your daily outlook?

Even people who are a lot better off spend time worrying about financial security. You may think, "that guy's making $80,000, $100,000, $125,000 a year. What's he got to worry about?" But the truth is that a lot of people who make those salaries, or a lot more, end up in financial ruin. That's because, while they may have a good job, they may not have financial discipline or a vision for how to live a fulfilled, financially vibrant life.

Whether you're rich or you're poor, it's nice to have money. It's even nicer to understand how to live so that you govern your money rather than letting it govern you. Whatever your income, your life will look vastly different when you achieve this level of control.

It's not impossible. It's absolutely achievable, and it starts by looking up!

Look up to that friend from high school who's managing his or her money well despite having a job that really doesn't pay all that much. Look up to that guy at work who has a financial plan and who continually executes on it. Look up to a financial advisor or coach who can guide you on what bills to pay today, what to pay over time, and how much of your income to move into savings or investments.

Your Life in Ten Years

Look up to the high-profile financial educators and programs that offer advice online, on TV, or in classes you can buy. Sure, they're out to make money, but that's not inherently bad. Much of what they recommend is based on sound financial theory, so as long as you study and do a bit of your own thinking, they can be worthwhile.

Look up to that high profile millionaire or billionaire – read his story and learn how he got started. That may be a way for you to get started, too!

Imagine your life in three years. Your credit cards are paid off. You have enough coming in to pay your monthly bills. Your emergency and vacation funds have money in them, you have a little in savings and a little in an investment or retirement account, growing while you live your life. You may not be wealthy, but just taking the first steps toward control of your finances can be a huge relief.

Now, imagine your life in ten years. Instead of worrying about paying off your credit cards, you've got a discretionary fund so large that it generates a monthly income!

You pay your monthly bills and your entertainment expenses with that income. You've set up an annuity that pays you a check for your once-a-year dream vacation. You have an established, disciplined program of first putting money into savings and then into investments. You meet with your financial advisor once each quarter to adjust your diversified investment portfolio for maximum growth, maximum income or maximum security, depending on where you are in life.

It's safe to say you're now as secure as most of us hope to be! Have you thought about what else that kind of security can get you?

When you don't have to worry about what will happen tomorrow, you'll find yourself much more relaxed. You'll be able to focus your attention on other important things, such as the quality of your life, how you treat people, your diet and fitness, and finding joy and success in what you do for a living. As you meet your own needs and those of your family, you'll be able to devote more of yourself and more of your money to personal fulfillment.

You can achieve those things you've always thought of as dreams – writing a book, traveling the world, running a super marathon, singing in musicals, or whatever your particular version of fulfillment may be. It's a very different picture than dragging yourself off to a job you hate every day, isn't it?

Take it to the Next Level

Look up to successful role models who resonate with you. Study their lives a bit to find out how they handle their own finances. Find out what they know and how they learned it. Take what you think will work in your circumstances and apply it. Pay attention to the results. If it's working, keep doing it. Refine it. Talk about it with your advisor or mentor. What lessons are you learning from your small successes, and how can you leverage them to get to a higher level?

If it's not working, try to understand why. Modify or tweak it to try to get it to work. If it simply doesn't work, abandon it and instead focus your efforts on other tactics that are successful.

Not sure how to leverage what you already know about money management to do even better? Look up!

Who's done this before, and what struggles did they have? Is anybody out there talking about how to solve your latest problem? We live in the richest information age in human history ... you can find answers to virtually any question if you take the time to search.

Look up, then set yourself up to move up.

What if you're doing okay and don't know what to do next? Not sure what the "next level" is? Look up! Who's playing the game at a slightly higher level than you? Are they talking about what they did to break through? Do your advisors or mentors have a track record of getting from where you are now to where they are? How did they do it? Ask them. Figure it out. Get coached and apply the advice to your own circumstances.

It's so important to get control of your financial life. When you're in control of your money, your daily life can look so much different! Instead of impulsively spending on whatever shiny object catches your eye, you have a plan – what to bills to pay, what to save, what to invest, what to set aside for that annual vacation, and what to put in the "fun fund."

Instead of turning away from or ignoring looming problems, you've got a plan for taking them on, so that even if you can't pay that bill off today or this month, you know how to settle it over the long term. You're proactive about contacting your creditors so that they're willing to work with you. You understand that when you need to raise a little more money than you get from your salary, you have a method in place like a second job, a consultation gig, or an online product to sell. Instead of worry, you have determination. Instead of doom and gloom, you have optimism.

Change and Challenge

Remember that when you look up (and start to move up), you'll be in a better position to help those around you. If you have family, they'll be better taken care of – better food on the table, a nicer place to live, more vibrant experiences daily and on those trips you can now afford to take. Not only that, you'll be a better role model – not just adored by your children and your spouse, but someone they can look up to as a role model for how to govern their finances. Money is a huge source of stress in many families. To reduce or eliminate that stress in yours, look up!

Will you struggle when you first start trying to implement this new approach? Of course! It may take you a few tries to get it right. Governing your finances is like a shower ... just because you took one today doesn't mean you don't have to take one tomorrow. Dust yourself off and try again!

Change and challenge aren't a part of life, they ARE life. But the guarantee is that if you do nothing, you'll be having the same problems next year that you're having this year. As we get older, our opportunities to make radical change can diminish. We have a smaller time period in which we can invest. Sometimes increased responsibilities make it harder to be financially nimble. There are lots of people who simply don't look up. They live impulsively in the moment. Their financial lives tend not to improve. Their vision is limited to what they've always done. They may wait too long and run out of time. Don't be one of those people.

Start today. Find your inspiration, find your role models. Dig in to figure out what they do that you need to do and take action. You CAN do it! Get control of your finances and change your life for the better.

You can start by looking up!

Notes

Notes

LOOK UP!

Set your sights high, the higher the better. Expect the most wonderful things to happen, not in the future but right now. Realize that nothing is too good. Allow absolutely nothing to hamper or hold you up in any way.

- Eileen Caddy

Eight - Are You Helping to Make the World a Better Place?

Are you frustrated by all the negative people in the news?

Does politics as usual make you want to give up?

Are you sick, sick, sick of seeing social injustice and ready to do something about it?

Do you believe change is possible when the right people come together with positive intentions?

Can you imagine a world where people are supportive of others regardless of their differences in language, nationality, race, religion, or economic status? It seems like people believe they should wait to make positive change until something changes in their own lives.

"I'll start speaking out against the gossip when I'm older."

"I'm afraid to voice my political opinions because I don't want to offend anyone."

"I'll go on a charity mission after I retire."

We're all busy, so it's not hard to understand why some folks think that way, but the truth is that, with the right inspiration, you can start helping the world today!

Imagine how grateful you would have been as a child if someone had stood up to that bully who was pestering you. Imagine the influence you could have in a local election if you work on the campaign of a positive, proactive candidate. Imagine the good you could do by being part of a social justice movement and insisting that the message stay rational, positive, and useful.

Imagine the richness of your own life if you put aside petty prejudices and actually develop friendships with people from countries and cultures other than your own. You can't put a price on that kind of wealth. It doesn't take a lot of money, a lot of time or a big resumé to start making the world a better place.

It starts by looking up!

Choose an Extraordinary Life

Look up to that one friend who seems able to understand both sides of an argument and find common ground in the middle. Look up to the rare politician in your community who advocates for his or her position without mud-slinging or personal insults. Look up to the successful business people like Warren Buffet and Bill Gates who donate some or all of their fortune to humanitarian organizations. Look up to the extraordinary people who have transcended humble beginnings and who can live comfortably anywhere in the world.

Look up to that part of yourself that feels grateful and connected. Live in that space.

Truly, we are what we think about, which is why looking up is so important. Be the change you want to see in the world. Create a life for yourself where the examples are good and helpful, so they'll inspire you to think about ways to make the world a better place. Get into conversations with positive, change-minded people. Read news stories or biographies featuring people who do the things you wish you could do someday. Reach out to the most prominent leaders in your community and find out how you can help. Choose to live a life of extraordinary unselfishness!

What Motivates You?

If you're motivated by financial gain, think about all the networking opportunities you can get by becoming a prominent advocate of positivity. If you're motivated by status, consider how important you'll be when people learn to think of you as someone who can navigate business or politics and light the way for improvement in your city, state, or nation. If you're intrinsically motivated, imagine the rich sense of contribution you'll get from working with a large group of people to bring about a more just, positive, and peaceful world.

Your message won't share itself. If you have a deep, passionate, live-giving message to share with humanity, remember this: the world needs what you have to offer.

There are so many people who could live a richly positive life but who never take action to change their reflexive negative thinking. There are wonderful calm people with a contributing mindset who don't feel that they could make a difference, so they leave public policy to the dreadful politicians who are all about mudslinging and personal enrichment. There are cause-minded people who watch from the sidelines because they're afraid of offending their friends or families ... when they could be thought leaders or influencers.

There are radiant, unique human beings trapped by their social conditioning, who believe that their message is too far outside the mainstream or that their ideas are not worthy of sharing. An important aspect of who these people are is wasted until they take action to start sharing their message and changing the world for the better.

Don't wait. It's time for you to get started. You can do good work. It's your time.

Get in the game by looking up!

Notes

LOOK UP!

Notes

LOOK UP!

Look up at the stars and not down at your feet. Try to make sense of what you see, and wonder about what makes the universe exist. Be curious.

- Stephen Hawking

Nine - Are You Vibrant?

Is there another level for you?

Do you feel trapped or somehow unable to truly express your energetic higher self?

Can you imagine living up to the amazing person that's inside you without being self-conscious, hampered by doubts or concerned about social judgment?

It's almost certain that you have more to offer the world, more action, more caring, more empathy, more energy, or more of all of these. It's also likely that something's holding you back, whether it's fear of failure, inhibition, expectations of others, doubts about your abilities, lack of energy, or simply not knowing how to get started. But living a vibrant life doesn't depend on money, social status, the positive judgment of friends, success at work, or anything other than you figuring out what allows you to live to your potential at this moment, then doing it.

To live a more vibrant, energetic life ... look up!

Would Your Days Look Different?

Look up to that friend or family member who always seems "switched on." Look up to the "go to" guy or gal at work who's always at the center of the most exciting projects. Look up to that one Facebook friend who always seems to be involved in the coolest events. Look up to the programs that help develop personal power or motivation. Look up to a high performance coach or mentor. Model your life after someone who plays at the highest levels of energy and engagement.

Imagine what it would be like to wake up knowing you were going to have an amazing day, that your attitude would be positive, your energy level high, and that whatever you encountered, you would meet it with self-confidence and joy! Would your days look different if you believed that you had more than enough personal resources to take on any problem? That your actions, when carefully considered and robustly executed, were right and just and did not depend on the approval of others? That you deserve happiness and that you can expect to have it every single day?

Imagine the power of moving through the world with that kind of vibrancy! Most of us spend at least part of every day just phoning it in or hesitating because we're worried about judgment or failure. What opportunities have you lost by not giving yourself confidently and joyfully to every moment? If you connected at the highest level with each and every thing you do, your results would be different, right?

You'd probably get more life out your interactions. You'd do better at work, complete your tasks with more expertise, interact on a higher level, and make better relationships. Most people would enjoy being around you more, but even if the full, true "you" isn't their cup of tea, they'd at least respect your energy and intensity.

Because your life would be rich and full, you'd do more giving. You'd have the energy and desire to exercise. Your financial decisions would be more carefully considered. You'd contribute to your community and to the world. You'd have a much, much better chance of feeling fulfilled when you're not limited by exhaustion, cynicism, or self-doubt.

A Million Reasons

Look up to people and circumstances that remind you to stay vibrant. Subscribe to a daily motivational post or podcast. Take a little time to have fun in places that leave you feeling light, refreshed, and open. Avoid cynical people and energy crushing activities. When you find that a person, program, or activity is draining your energy, think carefully about whether you're truly looking up to them. If you find that looking in their direction is actually looking down, shake them off, look around, find someone or something more energetically positive - even if it's yourself - and start looking up again!

There are a million reasons why people get stuck.

"I'm naturally pessimistic."

"I just went through a divorce."

"There are no good jobs out there."

"I tried being optimistic once and it didn't work."

None of these reasons should keep you from looking up, finding what you need to live an energetic, vibrant life, and doing it every single day. "Naturally pessimistic" just means you have a habit of negative thinking. Look up and learn to build a new habit. You deserve to be positive!

"Just went through a divorce" means you're still living in the past. It's time to look ahead and forge a new path. You deserve happiness!

"There are no good jobs out there" just means you haven't looked hard enough, long enough, or in the right places. If you can't find a job, you can always make one.

"I tried being optimistic once and it didn't work" just means you give up too easily. You may need a push – from a loving friend, from a motivational course, or from a coach or mentor.

"But I can't afford a life coach!"

Do you know how much wonderful, free motivation is out there, in library books, in church, on TV, and on the internet? We have access to more free information than at any time in the history of humankind. There's infinite learning available for very little effort. If you can't afford internet or a mobile phone, get your butt to the library and use the computers there!

Who Says You Can't Be Amazing?

If you've already done well, but now you're wallowing in the boredom of chasing the next expensive toy or distracting event, what's your excuse? "I'm too busy running my company." "Work's got me worn out." "My kids take up all my free time." Come on!

Who says you can't be energetic and have fun while running your company? If you're phoning it in, what kind of example does that set for your employees or coworkers? Do you take your kids to the park, then stick your face in your smart phone while they have the immersive experience you've secretly been craving?

Do you really believe that someone like you who's accomplished what you have is incapable of finding ways to get a little more vibrancy out of being outside for 45 minutes? Have you tried looking up?

There are so many who get this wrong. They start down the road of complacency, then find themselves trapped in boredom and fatigue. Daily drinking, smoking, staring at the TV, endlessly doing crossword puzzles, getting lost in Facebook for hours, making a life of shouting at political candidates in the news ... and then one day they find ten years have gone by and their lives haven't changed at all.

There's no reason to be afraid of joy, or to fail to seek more than you already have. You need energy to live a rich, full life, immersed in the moment, savoring the people and the experiences in your life. Time is running out, my friend!

Don't wait, make the decision to breathe more fully, to look more deeply into the eyes of your lover, to breathe the air more fully, to conquer your career or the company barrier that keeps you from where you want to be, to give yourself to a cause that nourishes your soul.

This much is true ... you can do better.

And it all starts by looking up!

LOOK UP!

Notes

Notes

LOOK UP!

Consult not your fears but your hopes and your dreams. Think not about your frustrations, but about your unfulfilled potential. Concern yourself not with what you tried and failed in, but with what it is still possible for you to do.

- Pope John XXII

Ten - Are You Fulfilled?

Are you barely getting through the days?

Are you working to pay the bills instead of building something important?

Does life sometimes seem like an endless series of tasks that don't relate to the things that fulfill you?

Would you give anything, almost anything, to feel like what you're doing truly matters?

It's been said that "sleep doesn't help if it's your soul that's tired." Another way to say that might be that if there's no sense of fulfillment in your life, it can be very hard to bring a lot of energy or passion to what you do. Each task seems like just another burden ... go to work, punch the clock, move some stuff around, sell this or that widget, put gas in your car, clean your house, grab some high-carb, low nutrition food, watch a few hours of TV, sleep fitfully, and get up to do it all again.

You drag yourself from one low yield activity to the next, hoping for distraction and pouring caffeine down your throat, hoping to regain some of your lost energy with stimulants because you're not getting it from a sense of meaning and purpose.

It doesn't have to be that way. When your days are driven by a sense of mission, when you have something meaningful to contribute, when you're inspired and most of your activity takes you closer to your dreams, that's where the magic happens. Instead of dragging yourself out of bed, you can hit the floor with energy, excited about what you get to do each and every day. Small tasks get done with speed and alacrity, and you get big chunks of your projects finished, immersed in your work, almost forgetting about the effort because you love both the process and the outcome.

The same sun rises and sets on your world as it does on everybody else's, but living a fulfilling life can make you feel like you're on a completely different planet. The universe is just as much aligned for success as it is for failure, but you can realign yourself and succeed wildly if you get pointed in the right direction and just keep moving!

It starts by looking up.

Excited About Your Mission

Look up to that friend who seems to take so much joy in his work. Look up to that co-worker who seems to love her job. Look up to the laborer who, regardless of the supposed low status of his or her profession, seems to take great joy in completing tasks, however menial – what may be looking down in "status" may actually be looking up when it comes to fulfillment! Look up to the entrepreneur who has started a company doing what he loves and who seems to have endless energy to create, promote, network, and build his business.

Look up to the CEO who's taken the reins of a company with challenges, embraced those challenges, and made it her personal mission to bring the company to profitability, sustainability, and contribution. Look up to the spiritual leader who's given up most of what you and I consider necessary but who still thrives while helping the disadvantaged, who seems not just to get through the days, but to radiate energy, who's a beacon of hope to humankind.

Imagine what life would look like if you woke up giddy with excitement about what you were about to do. Suppose your work was the thing you love to do, an activity that brought you health and joy, provided benefits to others, and generated a profit to fund your personal mission.

Think about the sense of satisfaction you'd get knowing that the work you do could actually make a difference in people's lives. Would taking the trash out and doing the weekly bookkeeping feel different if they were part of your mission of personal fulfillment, one that also happens to help the world?

You bet they would!

You can vector your days toward a much more fulfilling life when you start looking up to role models who inspire you to act in accordance with your higher self. You can make choices that build positive upon positive, heeding the angels of your better nature, moving you toward confidence, contribution and passion. Once you change your mindset, the feeling of your days will change. When you commit to acting in alignment with your goals and continue to take steps in the direction of your dreams, you'll be on the path to a much more fulfilling life.

Sure, there will be struggles. But, ask yourself this: why do people love the challenges of games so much? Part of it may be the camaraderie, but another part may be that we're actually wired to enjoy challenges. In games, the challenges are mostly manageable, and there's a clear reward at stake. Real life can sometimes be overwhelming. When there are too many challenges or when the challenges are too disconnected from our larger goals, we get frustrated.

If your challenges are overwhelming (or if you've shut down your life to avoid challenges) it may be that you simply need to clarify the connection between what you want out of life and how your challenges will help get you there.

You can start the process by looking up. Look up to the lifestyle you want. Look up to the people you want to emulate. Look up to the vision that you have for your legacy – what lessons and gifts you want to leave for your family and for the world. Look up to your creator and ask, "what work am I truly here to do?"

You probably know people who struggle with this, or who are failing at it. Some are stuck with the same problems they've had for years, hammering away at the same unrewarding job, frustrated at the same predictable social life, immersed in lukewarm relationships at home and at work. A lot of these folks fill their lives with TV, shopping, addictive video games, drinking or drugs. They seek the short term distraction – sometimes seem to revel in it – but don't seem to have any major life goals. Nor does their character seem to grow over the years. Do you know any of those people? Is there any chance that you may be one?

Each of us is given the extraordinary gift of life. We're born into different circumstances, we run into different struggles, we achieve different outcomes. But while we're here, we have the chance to revel in our time, to chase the fullness of life, whatever that may mean for each of us.

For you, it may mean getting control of your fitness and finances and spending your weekends flying small airplanes. It may mean that you find an energetic, positive life partner, start a family, and devote yourself to raising extraordinary children.

LOOK UP!

It may mean moving toward the top of your company, stepping into a high position at a competitor's company, and eventually running a business you love that both makes a profit and contributes to society.

It may mean that you give away all your possessions and wander the world. It may mean you devote yourself to helping less fortunate people. Or it may mean that you live a life that encompasses all these things!

It starts by looking up.

Are You Looking Up?

Are you looking up? Can you find role models to inspire you to take the steps you need to move in the direction of your dreams? Will you look for mentors to help you understand how to succeed at your mission?

Will you learn to listen to the better angels of your nature, the ones that suggest positive, productive choices and that urge you to look up, to step up, to reach up, to rise up and live into your highest self? Will you prepare yourself for a life of vibrancy and fulfillment by building habits that enrich you and help you get where you want to go in life?

Look up. Step up. Reach up. Rise up.

When you get there, give a hand up to someone who's in the position you were once in. Remember your own struggles and help them move up.

There's a different life waiting for you.

It can start, it does start, it *will* start when you start looking up!

Notes

Notes

LOOK UP!

I have faith in you. Every day can be a great day. Learn a lot, be nice to people, and most of all... have fun!

LOOK UP!

Nicklaus Suino is a martial arts expert, attorney, writer, and entrepreneur who specializes in the mastery process.

For more information please visit:
nicklaus-suino.com

Made in the USA
Monee, IL
01 April 2023

31045642R00069